Back To Normal

Dave Lordan & Karl Parkinson

Front Line Press

Published in 2022 by
Front Line Press
Copyright © Dave Lordan & Karl Parkinson

*"After one look at this planet any visitor from outer space
would say I want to see the manager."*

~William S. Burroughs.

Front Line Press

Contents

Undefeated

All those times
you thought you
bate me,
I let you win.

The bruises
you gave me
were only on
my skin.

My spirit untouched,
my record
unblemished in heaven.

I remain
undefeated,

champion of my own
indomitable will.

Photo

I looked at a photo of some long-gone friends and I
and saw my hair was thinning
then razored my crown, liberated from hair's flattery.

In those party dancing hours at discos with myself
I'm sometimes guested with departed friends.
Oh, how we sing and laugh at the caprices of destiny.

Postpandemic Prayer

Dear Sweet Jesus
with your sacred heart
bleeding for our loneliness

& for the love and honour of the Most High God

& in the smokey name of The Holy Spirit

& for the sake of the Queen of Heaven's starry Beatitudes

& for the memory of all those
who got help from St Anthony

& to help all the hopeless
who can't find St Jude

& in line with the grooviness of the New Groovy Pope

please let me be invited to a party

an absolute banger of a party

a total disgrace of a party

that goes on for days

in kitchens

& tents

& boreens

& ruins

& ends up in the woods

by a lough full of Loons

myself dancing like a rubber man

possessed by Grace Jones

surrounded by mad yokes

& sound heads

sharing Nirvana

we make for ourselves

for hours on end

Oh Lord for hours and hours and hours on end!

The Only Hero In Town

For some time I've been wishing

you did not exist

that I'd invented you

that you'd never barged

through our classroom door

with your fists clenched

and your heart on fire

roaring for our tyrant's blood.

I have wished you and wished you

and wished you again

out of my memory

out of my existence

out of my poetry

so that I wouldn't be scalded so often

by this unbearable, unnatural shame at my own

this unbearable insoluble shame

at the contrast twixt you (lanky & pale

& half-a-brit & only a blow-in)

and all those other red-faced men,

all those local, rebel-county men,

fatly descended from Heroes victorious,

who did not heroically storm into

our classroom in 1983

half-an-hour after their sons were bloody beaten

and lift the master by the neck

& pin him to the blackboard

and make him cry & beg

as he made children cry & beg
until he'd cursed their life for good

so that some of them lie now

forever-teen or twenty-something

in the same row in the graveyard

as you

who died in my eyes

& in the eyes of poetry died

guiltless and shining and old-heroic at your

appointed time, no earlier…

Oath To Back To Normal

whereby
schools shooting sex scandals
at 100 million fruit-picking lorry drivers
tricking hedge deals and bar room porn
filled with human prison blood
in the almighty corridors paved with trafficking rapes

and in accordance with
executioners migrating to the super market
to make wild fires crash into deadzones
and slaughter cattle that chainsaw the Amazon
while beating up queers out of digital spite

I do solemnly avow to sit and watch
the shortest country's Zoos explode as swarms of penguins
rise from the old Dutch well filled with drowning rhinoceri
in a stadium owned by a Florida cat shapeshifting
as the planet boils.

The Mysterious Mr Mangan

For Rob Doyle

A stranger in his country;

All whom he meets are demons out of the pit.

His father a human boa-constrictor.

His associates dishonour his person with their slime & venom.

The high, conical hat, the loose trousers many sizes too big for him,

and the old umbrella, so like a bagpipes.

He reads recklessly in many literatures.

The lore of many lands goes with him always.

He seems to seek in a world what is there in no satisfying measure or not at all.

None can say if it be pride or humility that looks out of that vague face.

Only his excesses save him from indifference - he seizes the keys of hell

and death, and flings them far out into the abyss,

proclaiming the praise of life.

A vessel of wrath

full of the ecstasy of combat

with the ardour of the wretched

with no native literary tradition to guide him,

can tell of the beauty of hate,

pure hate

as excellent

as pure love.

The Most Prestigious

Be wary for
in here you will find

Johnathan Slow
mocked up as Johnathan Swift.

Oscar Mild, not Oscar Wilde.

No James Joyce!
Bleedin
piles o' James Noyce!

And poor Clarence Mangled
by Lianne O Flattery
& Brian O Feel.

Look out! There's Billy-Butler Nomates
boring the eyebrows offa Edna Red Wine-Nose!

Take heed! Literary Journeyer from the lower ranks

for you are entering the scene of an ongoing crime

you will need all your wits to outlast;

keep your lips sealed
around Lady Narky-Snitch

& don't go anywhere lonesome
with Flan The Ham-Rhyme!

Restructuring

Of course, the ultimate benchmarking exercise is war
(Pentagon official)

Forget the friggin paint-ball.
Ayurvedic chanters-Take a hike!
I say to give the third floor EA's a taste
of real-world conditions.

Pack them off in a helicopter to Helmand.

See where their union guff will get them
in a sandstorm
under crossfire
at 46 degrees.

Let's hear the buggers bleating about pensions and insurance
when they've got to amputate their own limbs.

Won't that put a halt to their gallop!

Talk to the hand buddy, talk to the hand…tshh shh shh shh
or is it a foot? Hee-Hee-Hee…

Just one week
of natural selection
from the air
the market leader way

then the second interview, of course.

Think I'm nuts? I'm just on what someone somewhere
called the know
ledge
tough enough to look beyond
conception's precipice.

It's hot here.
The hot raw hand of the future is smacking my face!

Meeting At The Wake

Have you been long here, at The Wake?

I came here just a little while ago, straight from The Funeral.

How long has The Wake been going on for?

Nearly as long as The Funeral.

I saw people dropping dead over there at The Funeral.
I had to escape it.

They are dying here too at The Wake, boy.

Tell me, aside from ourselves, what kind of people
come to The Wake?

Whoever makes it through The Funeral.

And who is The Wake for?

Whoever doesn't make it through The Funeral.

The music is beautiful at the funeral, very affecting.

It is very affecting.

And this banquet. Fit for nobility.

It is too much, too costly.

The women look like they will never grow old.

They won't. Nor the men neither.

Are you sure this is really The Wake then and not The Funeral?

No, I am not!

Notice Of Cancellation

Your belongings will be stacked in

black sacks at the door

and there will be snipers on the roofs,

ARU in the bushes

should you try anything.

Your now ex will never ever utter

but may screech

your cursed name

when she's twisted.

Your Daddy will hardly creep

from the woodwork

like when you won

that award on TV.

Maybe there's a faraway island

that will have you.

Maybe down the line someone just

as taboo will embrace you.

Til then only pillows

to drown in

when you wake to the fear

in the dark.

So you might as well

fuck yourself

cut yourself

write yourself off

& we promise to gather

to piss on your plot,

celebrate victory; our not getting caught.

Toast To Back To Normal

To poisonous Salmon
and the rivers they don't
swim in.

To Blackrock Jocks
setting fire
to the junk-sick.

To the surgeries
recasting
the multitude's
faces.

To our daily disaster
and our therapeutic
shock.

To tragic incidents
on the line
at exactly
5 o clock.

The Man from Oblivia*

You know him.

He has no name

and no story to tell.

You know him.

He doesn't speak your language

or doesn't speak it well.

He brought an empty suitcase full of blank papers

and photographs of darkness.

He brought with him nothing

but trouble.

Sometimes he carries a shovel.

Sometimes a ticking clock.

Sometimes a deck of cards.

He sometimes straps magazines under his belt.

With him everything is a weapon.

Even the air scars as he opens it up walking through.

The killer ambulances,

the hospitals where zombies roam and children disappear,

the black dogs lepping

through cathedral doors,

the balls of lightening

passing through

the carriages of trains

are all down to him.

Those who live in palaces despise him most of all

and have sent a notice out: Surround him where you can,

strip him naked,

beat him like a dirty rug, pour tar on him, feathers.

Send him home.

*Years ago I heard an RTE newsreader misread 'A Bolivian Man' as 'An Oblivian Man'.

Talk Yaself Up

Do not tell dem yer unemployed

nor *between jobs* neitha,

don't talk no weasel tongue to dem.

Tell dem dat by high command

ya heard sung amidst Eugeanean Hills

by ancient Angel orators

psalming in the wind:

No soul can serve two masters

and to Babylon ya may not bend

therefore thou shalt not enter

dem mank satanic mills.

Sweet Tea Jingle

Don't wanna listen
to Rogan yappin
or Peterson preachin.

Don't care
who's twitterin
who's influencin who.

Don't wanna fight Jake Paul
or WAP
with Megan Thee Stallion.

Just wanna sit here in the sun
drinkin sweet tea
with you.

Normal Newsday

Another peacekeeper shoots
an old woman in the back.

Another Holy Joe's
a professional abuser.

Another rebel's transmuted
by power to a hack.

This youngfella's suicide.
That youngwan's car crash.

This tyrant over here.
That cyclone over there.

The very same
avoidable tragedies.

The very same
fatal absurdities.

Which is which?
Who is who?

This one screaming...
That one sighing...

Normal Service

The lifts are out of order,
coffee vendor's out of order,
the WIFI's out of order,
trams are out of order,
TV is out of order,
phonelines out of order.

Please sit tight & rest assured
your order's on the way.

Contact us if there's any delay.

Where's the order in Killiney?
Where's the order down in Sneem?
Where's the order up in Derry?
Where's the order in Dunquin?

Shelter in place, your order's on the way:

Contact Christ if there's any delay.

The dunes are disappearing,
the cliffs are sliding in,
vigilantes at the border
and no room at the Inn.

Remain at your location, your order's on the way.

Shove it up yer hole if there's any delay.

Angry Man On Twitter

He's an angry man on Twitter,
watch out, he'll get yuh if he can,
peepin through the blinds,
lookin for the Taliban.

He's an angry man on Twitter
somethin rotten in his head,
could be microchipped by Pfizer,
could be ergot on his bread.

He's an angry man on Twitter,
thinks the whole world's turning gay,
says the WHO are worse than Hitler,
the pandemic's just a play.

Golden harp - his profile picture.
Yiz bleedin hearts, yuh make him sick sure,
creepin on your Timeline
ta tell yiz how it is beor:

Yuh fuckin baby killin Muslim
Jewish tranny peedough tick,
Liberal atheist globohomo commie
brain washed bleedin prick whore!

Not Everyone Is Hitler Afterall

In the park with the sun on my neck
and the grass at my feet.
I don't see Hitler anywhere,
not the aulfella reading his paper,
not the nipper milling her ice cream,
not the ant trapezing the blade of grass,
not the quiet that squats on the hill
towards which I am moving, gladly.

Ancestry - The Results

I am 100% primordial quarksoup and here if you look, 100%
in a fog.

100% sure am I, aside from dreams and appetites,
that I follow
nothing
much
for sure atall.

At least 100% of my bloodline
is rich brown water from a bog.

My eyes are 100% the eyes
of the 10,000 grandmothers gathering.

I recall 100% of what they recall.

100% of my throat, my tongue is
for their unsung singing.

100% of my hands, like your hands,
are the hands I was dealt by biology.

100% of my bones,
like your bones,
will go to geology.

Sangha

Youthful multitudes murmurating
'round that hawthorn bush in Combray
and the wind blowing through it
and the skylarks singing.

Every great song,
and every great singer.

All the poets
in the trenches,
and the bedsits,
and the bookies,
and the cafes,
and the temples,
and the ruins,
and the forests,
and the caves.

The dew on the grass
in the moonlight in May.

This is my sangha.

Dug With Spoons*

Remember the ones who dug with spoons.
They dug & dug & dug with spoons.
They dug nights & they dug noons.
They dug they dug they dug with spoons.

They dug and as they dug they hummed.
They hummed because they couldn't sing.
They couldn't sing their people's songs.
Their nanas' songs their fathers' songs.

So they hummed and hummed their people-tunes,
their mother-tunes their father-tunes,
and dug until they left their cells
and tunnelled out through Empire's Hell
and hummed until the walls fell down
and thrust a dagger in the crown...

If for freedom you will to fight,
take heart from ones who spoon all night
and in deepest darkness strike for light!

Remember the ones who dig with spoons.
How they scoop through nights
& scrape past noons.
As they dig & dig & dig with spoons.
As they dig and dig and dig and dig!
As they dig and dig and dig and dig!
ALL NIGHT! WITH SPOONS!

*In tribute to various mass breakouts by political prisoners in Ireland, Palestine, and elsewhere, achieved with tiny secret repurposed implements like spoons - feel free to put a tune to it!

The Great Re-Opening

Sure it's great
to be back to normal,

to hourly extinctions,
and mosquitos in Cavan,

tropical nights
in November in Navan.

The Napalmist

The Napalmist has no eyes.
That's how he sees you.
Ridin so fuckin high up air
you won't even hear him boomin
when his levers slit the silver belly of the bomb whale
and a shoal of flashin silver mouths go raidin down.

Fall down.
Fall down.
Fall down.

And he has mouths to burn with.
So many snappin mechanical mouths to burn with,
to burn with, to burn with, to burn with.
His tongues have mouths to burn with.
His hair has mouths to burn with.
His chin has mouths to burn with.
His breasts are split by mouths.
His belly has a thousand rows of mouths.
His navel is one raw enormous mouth.
His spine is mouth upon mouth.
His cock and his balls are flaunting their mouths.

The Napalmist.
Hell is his Vegas.
Hell is his Carnival.
Hell is his Baby.
Hell is his Rosy Bouquet.
Hell is his Christmas Childhood.
And he'll suck the fuckin hell out of you

with all of his shimmerin mouths.
With his neck mouths.
With his wrist mouths.
His knuckle mouths.
His calf mouths.
His ear mouths.
His elbow mouths and his finger mouths
and his palm mouths.

But the mouths on the soles of his feet,
the mouths at the tips of his toes are the worst.

They'll give you a special kind of doom.
They'll snatch and clamp and crush and chew
and chomp and change the skin of all
the children of your neighbourhood,
chase them screaming naked from evaporated hearths
and up the melting road
with flames
stuck to them
like burning superglue.

News For The Dead

The situation in the land of the living
continues
to
deteriorate

& accelerate

as all that falls
and in line
with long-term expectations
now bearing fruit.

Expect at any moment
a sudden massive influx
of freshly fleeing souls.

Accordingly, clear the Lethe of
leisure-craft immediately
and evacuate the banks

the
many many miles of hinterland.

Chrysalis

The block where I outlived
my childhood is levelled.
My teenage home, rubble;
that mattress I lost my virginity on
in my grandparents' flat, ashes;
those paths we cut as we walked,
those streets we ran, not even ruins.

Your house is crumbling too, my friend
and all your lifetime's blocks and beds
are dust to come...

and tomorrow woods will sing
and woods will burn
and larvae in billions burst into wing
not caring for shedding
left to Wind, Sun,
and Withering.

Old Dog Love

What love is deeper than the Love of an Old Dog?

Where they have sailed with you, hey?

What storms they have seen you through, hey?

They know you girl. In the dim expiring candles of their eyes

they know about your vengeance and your love, they know
about your proverbs & your lies.

Inside & out, they know you.

Your causes are the currents in the drying oceans of their eyes.

Your triumphs burn like sapphire planets
in the cosmos of their eyes.

Their eyes.

Like blue moons rising over your sorrows.

Like blue suns on the horizons of your joys.

They know you, boy, they know that you are not just flesh &
bone, but passion also.

That you are steadfast in the passions of your heart.

They see the rose inside the stone inside your heart.

What can clasp you tighter inside its mighty failure
than the Love of an Old Dog?

LOVERS! You must look out for the rivers where the old dogs
lap their love!

Jiang Qing's Advice To The Young*

If good people beat bad people,
it serves them right;

if bad people beat good people,
the good people achieve glory;

if good people beat good people,
it is a misunderstanding;

without beatings,
you do not get acquainted;

with beatings you no longer need
to beat them.

*Translation of a quote from Jianq Qinq, who was Mao Zedong's 4th Wife
and a leading figure in the cultural revolution (1966-1976)

Grey Tablets

There are no grey ones.

There are speckled and striped, marbled and toned, stamped and engraved.

There are yellows and purples and reds, whites and blues and maroons.

Cylindrical greens, bullet shaped browns, blue UFO's .

Depending who's asking the question

I'll call them the Duchesses' Pearls,

I'll call them my Coral Medallions,

I'll call them my Found--on-the-Moon Beads,

my Gems-Washed-up-at-High-Tide,

my Quartz -from-the-Rainbow's-End.

There are no grey ones.

I gobble two yellows

to settle the shakes from the blues,

and a trio of whites to lap up the sweats

I get from the yellows.

I know that the lavenders tickle my heart

to keep it from dozing,

that the ruby-and-blues hoover up dirt in my veins,

that olives are flour to thicken the soup in my blood,

that mauves are riot police

scattering the mob in my head,

that greens nuzzle my eardrum and hum me to sleep,

that cherries send word to my throat

to remember to swallow the others.

Hold on there a minute till I catch my breath

and swallow a glass of water.

Tis a tablet for a tablet

and a pill for a pill

and sometime soon

I well get will.

Heh Tick!

If the very first time

y'eva protested

in yer life

woz wen u weren't

able ta go ta the boozer

for cuppla weeks

for the sake of d'elderly

de pregnant

de weak & de sick

Ya ain't no freedom fighter hunny

Yer an alcoholic.

Our Complaints Dept

Is located

on the 33rd floor

of eternity.

Its lines are open all the time

& you can leave a message anytime

anytime in eternity.

Maybe we'll get back to you sometime

sometime down the line

the line in eternity.

The Glass Sandwich.

for Robert Smith

I'm dead so it doesn't matter what I eat.

So I eat a glass sandwich
washed down with molten gold
at a hundred million degrees.

But it doesn't matter what I eat.
It really really doesn't matter what I eat.

So I eat geysers & magma.
I eat Netflix & the 19th century.
I eat Chopin & I eat a hearse.
I eat Honolulu & Hamburg & Uruk.

I eat the cartels & the Iranian Nuclear Programme.
I eat Caesar. I eat the sea peoples & the beaker people.
I eat the wolf that nursed Rome.
I eat Pandora in the womb.

Wash it all down with the raw egg of the sun.

And still it doesn't matter.
It really really really doesn't matter what I eat.

Hospice Earth

'What kind of monster is she who has eyes to see & ears to hear, and yet walks straight and does not despair?'
Killian Turner, Berlin Notebooks (1982)

As a thought experiment, imagine yourself in a mass of lemmings headed for the Cliffs of Moher.

If it helps, imagine the other lemmings in the mob being everyone you have ever known on first name terms - classmates, workmates, sessionmates, fuckmates etc.

Among the lemmings there are four broad groups:

The first group are the deniers. They deny the existence of the Cliffs of Moher. There is no Atlantic ocean either, according to them - after all, who has ever seen these supposed 'Cliffs', this ridiculous 'Ocean'?!

The green, lush, & rolling lands just continue forever, as does the going forward of the lemmings, & there is neither a need to nor a possibility of ever changing course, & to suggest otherwise is traitorous to lemmings.

This first group of lemmings is split in two, with some right up the front leading the charge towards oblivion as if it were heaven they were heading to, & some others guarding the very back, to stop any lemming trying to escape, (while secretly preparing their own escape, of course).

The second group, perhaps the most numerous, are only dimly aware or totally unaware that they are headed for the Cliffs of Moher.

They are just trotting along, living in the mindlessness of the moment, without any sense of how connected each moment is with all the moments that have come before & with all the moments that are yet to come.

Every passing breeze, every fart on the wind, distracts them; every drop of rain upsets them. They never meditate upon the cosmic absurdity of their origins, nor on the dark inevitability of their ends.

Then there are the optimistic lemmings. They are aware of the oncoming cliff but believe various things will mitigate the fall: for example that it is only a few feet of a fall. Maybe they will break an ankle, but that's about it.

Or they will sprout wings before they reach the edge of the cliffs.

Or there is a giant safety net, maybe even a gigantic trampoline at the bottom of the cliff and they will bounce back up & head back to yoga class, no bother.

The final group are the pessimists. They know it is a deathdrop, that there will be no miraculous mitigations, no sudden blooming of extra limbs, no safety net to protect from the jagged rocks & the seething depths.

Only the vast cosmos of the Atlantic, which will swallow all in an instant, without so much as a burp, & that will be that, for good.

The pessimists are few in number & for their own safety mostly keep mum.

Among the denialists, the innocents, & the optimists there pertains a visceral taboo against Despair - if any pessimists try & express their position they are mocked by an alliance of other groups & if they persist in their derangement they are accused (and therefore convicted) of crimes against lemmings and are trampled to death.

A few of the brightest optimists are actually pessimists who have decided it is more practical & perhaps even more honorable to go along, on the face of it, with the idea that it's all going to be grand & sure don't be worrying about it.

These we might call the pastoral lemmings. They see no point in terrifying those who are going to go over the cliff anyway however they are feeling or whatever they are thinking. These inverted pessimists simply want to help the others to die without them losing their minds first, & putting the awful truth in circulation will not help in this regard.

So they sing and whistle and crack jokes and put on little shows and so on & keep all the other lemmings in good spirits to the best of their ability, and as the cliff approaches they sing louder and louder and with more passion and eloquence and distractive power than ever before heard among lemmings.

Amidst all the other kinds of lemmings the pastorals feel - justifiably I think - that they are the only ones who are doing something demonstrably & practically useful for the collective, the only ones who truly understand what solidarity with & compassion for one's fellow-doomed might actually mean.

Relish & Triumph

With relish & triumph, the mouse downed the slug. The hedgehog devoured the mouse. The rat left not a molecule behind of the hedgehog. The fox inhaled the rat. The boar made fast food of the fox. The man shot the boar. Which made a fair few fleas homeless. Briefly, for they soon alighted on the man, who had a long full beard & a lovely hairy back for them to settle into snugly. They felt like they had moved just like that from a hovel to a mansion - rags to riches in one glorious instant! But that didn't last long either, for the man barbecued the boar for his birthday a few days later & fed it in chops & burgers to a long line of family & friends & then he died along with all the rest of them from a virus passed on from the slug & so the fleas moved on & so did the virus & that's not the end of it either. Oh no it isn't!

Scenic Parable

For FBBOABW

I have a friend whose father was a traveling conman who had once gotten by for a year or two selling personal hygiene products out of the boot of his car to service stations and corner shops and the like. His method was simple, obvious, and effective. The father's mate in the recycling centre sold the father lots of emptied & discarded big brand containers for shampoo and conditioner on the cheap, and then the father refilled those with the very cheapest bulk-buy shampoo and conditioner from the Euro-stores. The garages and so on thought they were getting premium products at basement prices, and sold them on at massive mark-ups to unwitting consumers. This was fool-proof as long as it lasted, which was until the mate eventually moved on from the recycling centre. In the meantime no-one among the staff, management, or customers of hundreds of family-sized retail outlets the length and breadth of Ireland ever noticed a thing, or if they did they said nothing about it.

Brief credo based on a sentence of Carver's

Not only *to write*
but to try and *live*
a little
every day

without hope
and
without despair

confessing the artful animal you are

and couldn't be

otherwise

steadfastly, solemnly in love
with that last receding
particle
of antique light

so miniscule, so imperceivable a photon now
it has to be conjured, imagined,
theorised...

Poets Advertisement

Those strategic fools, those PR goons, those
innocent gobs thinking they're selling us,

sell only passports to a dammed Gombeen nation
stamped with their own made-up faces.

Hell is stock and trade of every big business -
no poet will shill for McDonalds, or pimp for Aer Lingus.

True Rhymers breathe free inspiration - our brand, eternal,
unsellable - The Great Name Anonymous.

Who Are These Poems For

The people of the favelas, tower blocks,
barrios, ghettoes, slums, trailer parks,
halting sites, the Misérables, the mad, the wild,
the wounded,
the weary,
the wicked,
the sick,
the damaged
the addicted,
the survivors.

For bar staff and barflies, shoplifters and shop assistants,
baristas and butchers and gas dealers and crack sellers.

For the shamed, the savage and the scared,
the dangerous and demented,
the salt of the earth and the sour faced,
the know not what they do, the unwilling and unwanted,
the rabble and the mob,
the many and the few, the malignant and maligned,
the forgotten, the downtrodden
the done up, the sexed up, the seductive,
the sinful and sinned on, the mean,
the murderous, the heroic and the holy,
the countless beings in the coming and going

and toing and froing, in the endless aeons of samsara;
may you be free from suffering.

You who read this now, these poems are for you.

The Sky Road

The Lords and Leaders o this Earth

want me to blank out me nana's face,

forget all me granda's suffering and joy,

piss on me auld aunty's grave,

and me answer is no!

I rest me cheeks in me nana's lap.

I tarry me granda's green sleeves.

I'm nursed by the springs

where me auld aunty bathes.

The Lords of a Day

and the Leaders of a Week

are innocent of the grander course,

the route that links the mountain

to the sky.

For Diego

In Memory of Diego Maradona 1960-2020.

Diego, you were the summer at its zenith,
the perfect day in its perfect hour.
You, mercurial slum *Indian*
who slalomed through defenses with magistral elegance.

You, dynamo of danger, a five-foot five-inch giant,
no eye could blink at the sight of your scintillating movement,
your divine left foot, like some genie sprung from a lamp
granting wishes to the crowds of Boca, Barca, Napoli,
your beloved Argentina, Argentina, Argentina!

And I will not hear talk of the drugs you took,
nor the flaws you had,
nor the things they say you wasted...

No, I only want to watch you over and over again
defeating the English team in 86, the hand of God,

the feet of Hermes, the audacity of genius,

show me once more that turn on the half way line

before setting off on the goal of the century,

hang it on a wall beside Picasso or Monet,

for it too is a great work of art…

No don't preach to me

about his off-field activities,

oh put down your stones,

and listen to the chant of the Neapolitans,

only show me that image of you

in a blue and white striped jersey,

holding aloft that shining gold statue, your smiling face,

and Italy is beaten, and England is beaten,

and Belgium is beaten, and Germany is beaten,

and Diego Armando Maradona is the champion of the world.

Spitting On Another Master's Grave

It was bright October in our holy school
& the dazzle
of afternoon was sowing
light-headedness throughout
our classroom. Even the master was smiling.
Smiling at us with amused eyes
& telling some rambling tale
from a campfire of his youth,
the same one he recounted
whenever a smile spread across his face like a crack in a grave.
It put us all
in a celebratory, open-hearted mood.

Somehow the master got on to The Milky Way,
which he declared a star.
Up I piped, Sir! Sir!
Sir! Sir! Sir! piped I.
The Milky Way is not a star, it's a galaxy.
This he, irritated, refused to accept,
nor would I condescend to backdown,
until it was time to appeal to Old Authority.
So the master donned his reading spectacles and selected
Britannica volume M-L from his one shelf of The
Enlightenment &, back turned to us, buried his snout in it.

Two minutes later he swung around inflamed & roughly roared
at us to get out our
Irish books...

...Next day in our holy school, dedicated to The Virgin,
blessed by many bishops, the master approached my desk
at the front of the class, which I shared with another 9-year-old
boy, in a room full of 9-year-old boys.
He was gripping an ant between finger & thumb.
He deposited the ant in front of me on the desk.
He then pointed at the ant & said,
What's that in front of you Lordan? Cad é seo, ha?
I stuttered, not knowing what to say.
Not knowing what was up. The master picked up the ant &
held it to his right eye to examine it. *Nits* he announced. *You've
got nits you dirty animal, so many nits they're hopping onto the desk.*
Then the master held the ant up & out towards the classroom
the way to give them all a good gawk and confirm his
discovery. And there was an uproar of cruel, callous
merriment at my expense that lasted for many months.

My nickname for the rest of that year was Nits. I heard it every
day a thousand times. Shouted at me in the corridor, chanted at
me in the yard, whispered about me in the line, inked about
me on every toilet door in the school.   *Nits Nits Nits Nits*...I
was the spittoon of that classroom - everyone hawked their

poison up on me. It nearly drove me to suicide at 9 years of age.

And yet, it's not me that's dead. It's not me that's shamed. It's not me that stands eternally condemned. It's him. Once he was briefly my destiny. Now I am permanently his. And the Milky Way is still a galaxy, not a star. And a master is still only a master. And a poet, even at 9 years of age, still infinitely greater.

I am the smile that cracks your grave face now cruel master. And I laugh a laugh that is much much crueler. My spit is in your mouth, forever, and you may slurp it cold from here on in until stars become galaxies, until bishops are holy, until wine turns into blood.

Master, I am the rift in your memory now. Unsealable for good.

Gautama's Smile

All was drowned or turning in the flames,

and the vision laughing repudiated me,

but I returned with Gautama's smile

and winking I walked

into the garden eternal

and waiting there for me

auld Walt and William B.

Acknowledgements

We would like to thank our families, friends and readers for their ongoing support of our creative endeavors.

We would like to thank PoetryIreland for awarding us a Poetry Town Bursary in 2021, which went a long way to helping us complete the writing of this book.

Some poems included here were previously published by *The Survivors Trust*, by *Beir Bua Journal*, by *Translation – The Art of Possibility*, & in *Correspondences – Anthology to call for an end to Direct Provision.* Our thanks to all the editors.

Dave Lordan is the author of the poetry collections **The Boy in the Ring** (2007), which won the Patrick Kavanaugh Award, the Shine/Strong Award, and was shortlisted for the *Irish Times* poetry award, **Invitation to a Sacrifice** (2010), and **Lost Tribe of the Wicklow Mountains** (2014), all published by Salmon Poetry, and **Medium** (Front Line Press 2020). Wurmpress published his short story collection **First Book of Frags** in 2013. His play *Jo Bangles* was produced by the Eigse Riada company in 2010. In 2011 Lordan received the Ireland Chair of Poetry Bursary. He is contributor to Arena, the arts program for RTE. His writing has been published widely, including: *The Stinging Fly, Granta, RTE Culture, Poetry, The 32, The Cry of the Poor,* Dave is well known for his multimedia work in poetry film, videography and performance.

Karl Parkinson is a writer from inner-city Dublin. **Sacred Symphony** his third collection of poetry was published in 2020 by Culture Matters. His second collection of poetry, **Butterflies of a Bad Summer**, was published in 2016 by Salmon Poetry. His début novel, **The Blocks**, was published in 2016 by New Binary Press. In 2013 Wurmpress published his début poetry collection, **Litany of the City and Other Poems**. His work has appeared in the anthologies, *New Planet Cabaret* (New Island Press), *If Ever You Go: A Map of Dublin in Poetry and Song* (Dedalus Press), *The deep Hearts Core: Irish poets revisit a touchstone poem* (Dedalus Press), *Even The Daybreak: 35 years of Salmon Poetry*, *The Children of the Nation: An Anthology of Working Peoples Poetry From Contemporary Ireland* (Culture Matters), as well as in several journals and newspapers, including *The Stinging Fly*, *The Irish Times*, *Penduline* (USA), *Dublin Inquirer* and many more. Karl is one of Ireland's most acclaimed live literature performers. His work has been broadcast on national TV and Radio.

Printed in Great Britain
by Amazon